EXPLORE THE UNITED STATES

INDIANA

Julie Murray

Big Buddy Books

An Imprint of Abdo Publishing
abdobooks.com

abdobooks.com

Published by Abdo Publishing, a division of ABDO, PO Box 398166, Minneapolis, Minnesota 55439.
Copyright © 2020 by Abdo Consulting Group, Inc. International copyrights reserved in all countries.
No part of this book may be reproduced in any form without written permission from the publisher.
Big Buddy Books™ is a trademark and logo of Abdo Publishing.

Printed in the United States of America, North Mankato, Minnesota
102019
012020

THIS BOOK CONTAINS
RECYCLED MATERIALS

Design: Aruna Rangarajan, Mighty Media, Inc.
Production: Mighty Media, Inc.
Editor: Liz Salzmann

Cover Photograph: Shutterstock Images
Interior Photographs: Adam Lacy/Icon Sportswire/AP Images, p. 18; Bart Everson/Flickr, p. 9 (left);
    Chapsam/Wikimedia Commons, p. 29 (bottom right); Chris M Morris/Flickr, pp. 10, 11; Daniel
    Dempster Photography/Alamy Stock Photo, p. 28 (top); Elise Amendola/AP Images, p. 23; Jeremy
    Hogan/AP Images, p. 17; Jessica Hill/AP Images, p. 19; John L Hendricks/AP Images, p. 28
    (center); John T Daniels/Wikimedia Commons, p. 21; Larry C. Lawson/AP Images, p. 29 (top right);
    Library of Congress, p. 20; MICHAEL S. GREEN/AP Images, p. 13; NADEJDA2015/iStockphoto,
    p. 30 (top left); Shutterstock Images, pp. 4, 5, 6, 7, 9, 11 (inset), 14, 15, 16, 22, 24, 25, 26, 27, 28,
    29, 30; Tom Strickland/AP Images, p. 27 (top); Tomasso DeRosa/AP Images, p. 29 (top left); White
    House Historical Association/Wikimedia Commons, p. 26 (bottom left); Wikimedia Commons,
    p. 26 (bottom right)

Populations figures from census.gov

Library of Congress Control Number: 2019943336

Publisher's Cataloging-in-Publication Data
Names: Murray, Julie, author.
Title: Indiana / by Julie Murray
Description: Minneapolis, Minnesota : Abdo Publishing, 2020 | Series: Explore the United States |
    Includes online resources and index.
Identifiers: ISBN 9781532191176 (lib. bdg.) | ISBN 9781532177903 (ebook)
Subjects: LCSH: U.S. states--Juvenile literature. | Midwest States--Juvenile literature. | Physical
    geography--United States--Juvenile literature. | Indiana--History--Juvenile literature.
Classification: DDC 977.2--dc23

CONTENTS

ONE NATION

The United States is a diverse country. It has farmland, cities, coasts, and mountains. Its people come from many different backgrounds. And, its history covers more than 200 years.

Today the country includes 50 states. Indiana is one of these states. Let's learn more about Indiana and its story!

DID YOU KNOW?
Indiana became a state on December 11, 1816. It was the nineteenth state to join the nation.

Lake Michigan is on Indiana's northwest border. It is one of the five Great Lakes.

CHAPTER 2

INDIANA UP CLOSE

The United States has four main regions. Indiana is in the Midwest.

Indiana has four states on its borders. Michigan is north and Ohio is east. Kentucky is south and Illinois is west. Lake Michigan is on Indiana's northwest corner.

Indiana has a total area of 36,420 square miles (94,327 sq km). About 6.7 million people live in the state.

Puerto Rico became a US commonwealth in 1952.

DID YOU KNOW?

Washington, DC, is the US capital city. Puerto Rico is a US commonwealth. This means it is governed by its own people.

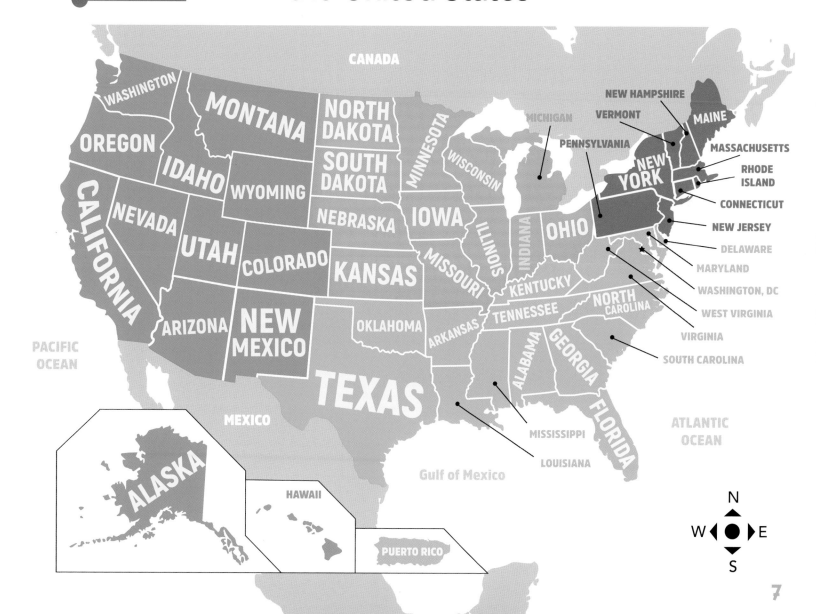

Regions of the United States

West
Midwest
South
Northeast

CANADA

WASHINGTON
MONTANA
NORTH DAKOTA
SOUTH DAKOTA
MINNESOTA
WISCONSIN
MICHIGAN
NEW HAMPSHIRE
VERMONT
MAINE

OREGON
IDAHO
WYOMING
NEBRASKA
IOWA
PENNSYLVANIA
NEW YORK
MASSACHUSETTS
RHODE ISLAND

CALIFORNIA
NEVADA
UTAH
COLORADO
KANSAS
MISSOURI
ILLINOIS
INDIANA
OHIO
CONNECTICUT
NEW JERSEY
DELAWARE

ARIZONA
NEW MEXICO
OKLAHOMA
ARKANSAS
KENTUCKY
TENNESSEE
NORTH CAROLINA
MARYLAND
WASHINGTON, DC
WEST VIRGINIA
VIRGINIA

TEXAS
ALABAMA
GEORGIA
SOUTH CAROLINA

MISSISSIPPI
LOUISIANA
FLORIDA

PACIFIC OCEAN

MEXICO

ATLANTIC OCEAN

Gulf of Mexico

ALASKA

HAWAII

PUERTO RICO

N
W E
S

7

IMPORTANT CITITES

CHAPTER 3

IMPORTANT CITIES

The capital and largest city of Indiana is Indianapolis. It is home to 867,125 people. It is called the "Circle City" because of its layout.

The city hosts important sports events. Cars race at Indianapolis Motor Speedway. And, the Indianapolis Colts play football at Lucas Oil Stadium. In 2012, the stadium hosted the Super Bowl for the first time!

FORT WAYNE has been named an All-American City three times! Only ten US cities receive this honor each year.

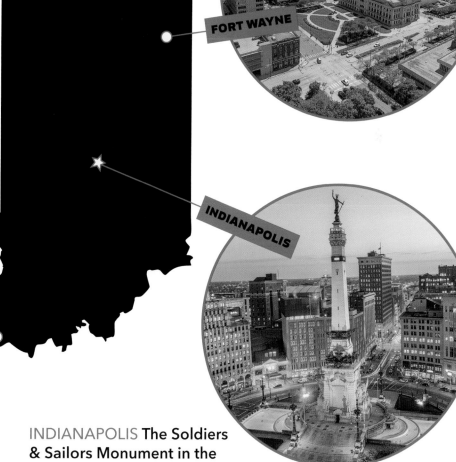

FORT WAYNE

INDIANAPOLIS

EVANSVILLE

EVANSVILLE Angel Mounds State Historic Site is near Evansville. Native Americans built a town there more than 500 years ago.

INDIANAPOLIS The Soldiers & Sailors Monument in the center of the city honors war heroes. It is on the National Register of Historic Places.

Wesselman Woods Nature Preserve is in Evansville. It is a National Natural Landmark and the largest original forest inside any US city limits.

Fort Wayne is the second-largest city in Indiana. It has 267,633 people. This city is located where the Saint Marys and Saint Joseph Rivers meet. They join to form the Maumee River.

Indiana's third-largest city is Evansville, with 117,963 people. It is located on the Ohio River.

CHAPTER 4

INDIANA IN HISTORY

Indiana's history includes Native Americans and settlers. Native Americans lived in the area first. In 1679, French explorers arrived by boat. Soon, settlers came to stay. In 1800, the Indiana Territory was created.

In the early years, settlers and Native Americans fought often. After the fighting lessened, Indiana became a state in 1816.

In the 1900s, Indiana became known for making steel. Tens of thousands of people worked in Indiana's steel mills by the 1920s.

In the 1900s, Gary was a major steel-producing city.

CHAPTER 5

ACROSS THE LAND

Indiana has hills, lakes, and rich farmland. Sand dunes are found along Lake Michigan. The Wabash River is a major waterway in the state.

Many types of animals make their homes in Indiana. These include raccoons, rabbits, woodchucks, and ducks.

DID YOU KNOW?

In Indiana, the average high temperature in July is 85°F (29°C). In January, it is 35°F (2°C).

The Wabash River flows
from Ohio through Indiana.

CHAPTER 6

EARNING A LIVING

Manufacturing, finance, and health care businesses provide jobs in Indiana. Important products include chemicals and automobile parts.

Another important Indiana business is farming. Major crops include corn, soybeans, mint, watermelons, and tomatoes.

Large amounts of limestone are found in southern Indiana. The state also mines coal and clay.

DID YOU KNOW?
New York City's famous Empire State Building was built using Indiana limestone.

Its uniform quality makes Indiana limestone some of the best in the world.

CHAPTER 7

SPORTS PAGE

Many people think of sports when they think of Indiana. The Indianapolis Colts football team and the Indiana Pacers and Fever basketball teams have many fans. College basketball is also very popular!

Indiana is known for car racing too. The Indianapolis 500, or Indy 500, takes place every year. Top drivers from around the world take part in this famous race.

DID YOU KNOW?

The winning team of the Indy 500 kisses the brick finish line. This practice started in 1996.

Tamika Catchings was a star player on the Indiana Fever basketball team from 2002 to 2016. She helped the team win the WNBA Championship in 2012!

CHAPTER 8

HOMETOWN HEROES

Many famous people are from Indiana. Wilbur Wright was born near Millville in 1867. He and his brother Orville are famous inventors. Together, they made the first successful airplane!

On December 17, 1903, Orville flew their airplane near Kitty Hawk, North Carolina. This was the first successful flight. Later that day, Wilbur flew 852 feet (260 m) in about one minute. This was their longest flight that day.

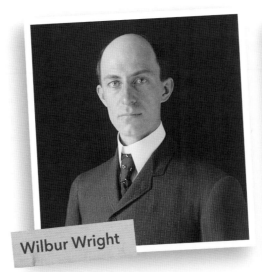

Wilbur Wright

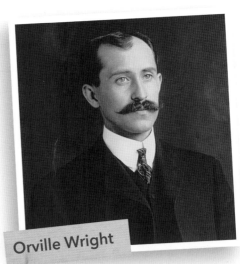

Orville Wright

Orville Wright flew the Wright Flyer for the first time. This plane was powered and could be controlled.

Larry Bird was born in West Baden in 1956. Some say he is one of the greatest basketball players. He became known for having skills in many areas of the game.

Bird played for Indiana State University from 1976 to 1979. He played for the Boston Celtics from 1979 to 1992. After Bird stopped playing, he coached the Indiana Pacers from 1997 to 2000.

DID YOU KNOW?

Janet Jackson was born in Gary and grew up in a musical family. She is known for songwriting, singing, and dancing. Jackson entered the Rock & Roll Hall of Fame in 2019.

Bird helped lead the Celtics to three NBA Championships.

CHAPTER 9

A GREAT STATE

The story of Indiana is important to the United States. The people and places that make up this state offer something special to the country. Together with all the states, Indiana helps make the United States great.

There is a lot of beauty throughout the state of Indiana.

Indiana Dunes State Park is located along Lake Michigan. Some of its sand dunes are almost 200 feet (61 m) high!

TIMELINE

1816

Indiana became the nineteenth state on December 11.

1800s

1889

Standard Oil Company built one of the world's largest refineries in Whiting.

Past Indiana Territory governor William Henry Harrison became the ninth US president. He died 30 days later.

1841

Elwood Haynes invented one of the first gasoline-powered cars in Kokomo.

1894

1911

The first Indianapolis 500 race took place at Indianapolis Motor Speedway.

2007

The Indianapolis Colts football team won the forty-first Super Bowl!

2017

Indiana native and governor Mike Pence became vice president of the United States.

1900s

2000s

Dan Quayle of Indianapolis became vice president of the United States.

1989

Indianapolis hosted the forty-sixth Super Bowl.

2012

TOUR BOOK

Do you want to go to Indiana? If you visit the state, here are some places to go and things to do!

LISTEN

Hear some bluegrass music. There are several bluegrass festivals held in the state each year. Bluegrass bands often include fiddles, banjos, and mandolins.

TASTE

Munch on popcorn and visit the Orville Redenbacher statue at Valparaiso's annual popcorn festival. Redenbacher was born in Brazil, Indiana.

Try a famous Indiana pork tenderloin sandwich.

CHEER

Indiana is known for having many basketball fans. Watch an exciting game at Indiana University!

The men's and women's basketball teams both play in Simon Skjodt Assembly Hall.

LEARN

Indiana is home to many Amish people. They are known for living simply and free of modern things. Visit Amish Acres in Nappanee to see how they live.

EXPLORE

Visit Cataract Falls in Cloverdale. It is the largest waterfall in Indiana!

FAST FACTS

▶ STATE FLOWER
Peony

▶ STATE TREE
Tulip Tree

▶ STATE BIRD
Northern Cardinal

▶ STATE FLAG:

▶ NICKNAME:
Hoosier State

▶ DATE OF STATEHOOD:
December 11, 1816

▶ POPULATION (RANK):
6,691,878
(17th most-populated state)

▶ TOTAL AREA (RANK):
36,420 square miles
(38th largest state)

▶ STATE CAPITAL:
Indianapolis

▶ POSTAL ABBREVIATION:
IN

▶ MOTTO:
"Crossroads of America"

GLOSSARY

capital—a city where government leaders meet.

chemical (KEH-mih-kuhl)—a substance that can cause reactions and changes.

diverse—made up of things that are different from each other.

dune—a hill or ridge of loose sand piled up by the wind.

limestone—a type of white rock used for building.

region—a large part of a country that is different from other parts.

ONLINE RESOURCES

Booklinks
NONFICTION NETWORK
FREE! ONLINE NONFICTION RESOURCES

To learn more about Indiana, please visit **abdobooklinks.com** or scan this QR code. These links are routinely monitored and updated to provide the most current information available.

INDEX